D0568182

# A New True Book

# PIONEERS

By Dennis B. Fradin

CHILDREN'S PRESS™
CHICAGO

Wagon trains carried settlers west
across North America.

PHOTO CREDITS

Australian Information Service—10

Bettmann Archives, Inc.—33

The Granger Collection: Cover, 6 (four
photos), 9 (top left), 20 (top left), 23, 25,
27, 28 (two photos), 35 (top left), 37 (top
right), 43

Historical Pictures Service, Chicago: 2, 9
(top right), 15, 20 (top right), 22, 26, 31, 35
(top right), 37 (top left), 38, 39, 41

NASA—45

©Jim Rowan—18 (bottom)

State of Florida, Department of
Commerce—Division of Tourism—18 (top)

U.S. Department of Interior-NPS photo by
Fred Bell—4

Tom Dunnington—13

Cover: The Pioneer's Home on the
Western Frontier, lithograph, 1867 by
Currier & Ives

Library of Congress Cataloging in Publication Data

Fradin, Dennis B.
    Pioneers.

    (A New true book)
    Summary: Discusses the reasons people had for
going to live in newly-discovered or newly-settled
lands, as the American West of the nineteenth century,
the hardships they faced, and their influence on
history.
    1.   Pioneers—History—Juvenile literature.
2.   Explorers—History—Juvenile literature.   3.   Frontier
and pioneer life—History—Juvenile literature.
4.   Pioneers—United States—Juvenile literature.
5.   Frontier and pioneer life—United States—
Juvenile literature. [1.   Pioneers.   2.   Frontier and
pioneer life]   I.   Title.
GF53.F73   1984        910′.92′2        84-9418
ISBN 0-516-01927-9            AACR2

Copyright© 1984 by Regensteiner Publishing Enterprises, Inc.
All rights reserved. Published simultaneously in Canada.
Printed in the United States of America.
    2 3 4 5 6 7 8 9 10 R 93 92 91 90 89 88 87 86 85

# TABLE OF CONTENTS

Settlers moved on foot and horseback across the Cumberland
Gap connecting Kentucky and Tennessee.

# WHAT ARE PIONEERS?

People who are among the first to move into a new place are called pioneers. The word *pioneer* comes from a Latin word meaning "foot." When the word was first used, pioneers usually traveled on foot.

There have been pioneers for as long as there have been people. Thanks to pioneers, human beings now live in almost every part of the world.

Vasco da Gama (top left) received a blessing from King Manuel I
of Portugal before he left on his 1497 sea voyage to India.
Ponce de Leon (top right) and his men searched for the Fountain
of Youth in Florida. Columbus (below left) and his sailors landed
on the island of Hispaniola. LaSalle (below right) traveled
down the Mississippi River to the Gulf of Mexico.

# WHY DO PEOPLE BECOME PIONEERS?

The first persons to visit a new place are called explorers. Explorers usually return home and talk about the places they have seen. Some people decide to live in these new places. Those people are pioneers.

Why face the hardships and dangers of moving to

a new place? Hunger is one reason. There have always been people without enough to eat. New places with good hunting, fishing, or farmland look good to poor, hungry people.

People often have moved to far-off places so they could worship freely. The Pilgrims left Europe and came to America to have religious freedom.

After 1848 thousands of people went to California to look for gold.

Gold and other riches have also made people want to go to far-off places. After gold was found in California in 1848, hundreds of thousands of people moved there.

Some people did not want
to be pioneers. Outlaws
and losers of wars have
been forced to leave home
and settle elsewhere.
People in overcrowded

First convict colony at Sydney Cove in Australia. Britain sent
men and women who had broken the law to Australia as punishment.

countries also have been forced into pioneering.

Even in places that are not overcrowded, there are always those who want more elbowroom. Daniel Boone was one such pioneer. Boone once joked to his wife that they had to move. Someone had settled seventy miles away, making the place too crowded!

There are other reasons why people have become pioneers. Farmers, storekeepers, and others are needed in newly settled lands. They have a good chance to make a living there. A new place also means a fresh start for those who want to forget the past. Finally, isn't there something exciting about being among the first to live in a new place?

# ANCIENT PIONEERS

More than a million
years ago, the first people
lived in Africa, Asia, and
Europe. While searching for
food, early people explored
new lands.

Some prehistoric pioneers traveled far. Among those were the Indians, who came to America from Asia more than twenty thousand years ago. It is thought that the Indians walked to present-day Alaska over a land bridge that no longer exists.

Once in North America, the Indians walked across present-day Canada and the United States. Then

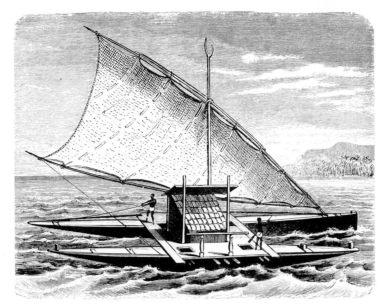

Double canoes were used by the people of Fiji.

they moved south into Central and South America.

Early pioneers also traveled by water. Two thousand years ago Polynesian people left their homes. They sailed for thousands of miles across the Pacific Ocean. Some

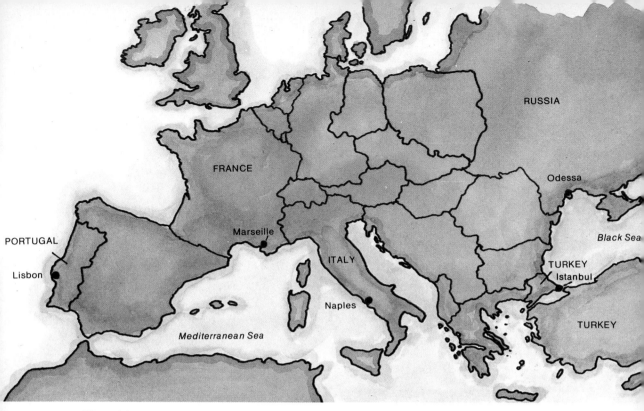

The cities shown above were founded by the ancient Greeks.

landed in the Hawaiian
Islands and stayed.

The ancient Greeks were
important pioneers. Greek
pioneers founded cities in
Portugal, Italy, Russia,
Turkey, and France.

16

Ancient pioneers helped shape the way of life in places they settled. For example, Gaelic has been spoken in Ireland since the Celts brought the language there twenty-four hundred years ago. Polynesian settlers named Hawaii after their ancient homeland— Hawaiki. Life in Korea and Vietnam was shaped by Chinese who settled there long ago.

The oldest wooden schoolhouse (above) in the United States is in
St. Augustine, Florida. The Castillo de San Marcos was built in
1672. It is the oldest stone fort in the United States.

# PIONEERS IN AMERICA

Much of America's history is the story of pioneers moving to new places.

The first permanent settlement in what is now the United States was built by Spaniards in St. Augustine, Florida, in 1565. However, the English were the main settlers of America.They built the first permanent English settlement at Jamestown,

19

TAYLOR HICKS SCHOOL LIBRARY
PRESCOTT, ARIZONA

These engravings show the pioneers building Jamestown (left) and early settlers trading goods with the Indians (right).

Virginia, in 1607. By the late 1600s there were English settlements all along the eastern coast. The rest of the country belonged to the people who had lived there for twenty thousand years—the Indians.

| Colony | First Permanent Settlements | Date |
| --- | --- | --- |
| Virginia | Jamestown | 1607 |
| Massachusetts | Plymouth | 1620 |
| | Salem | 1626 |
| | Boston | 1630 |
| New Hampshire | Portsmouth | 1623 |
| New York | Fort Orange | 1624 |
| | New Amsterdam | 1626 |
| New Jersey | Jersey City Region | 1630 |
| Maryland | St. Mary's | 1634 |
| Connecticut | Connecticut Valley | 1633-36 |
| Rhode Island | Providence | 1636 |
| Delaware | Fort Christina | 1638 |
| North Carolina | Albemarle Sound | 1653-60 |
| South Carolina | Charles Town | 1670 |
| Pennsylvania | Philadelphia | 1682 |
| Georgia | Savannah | 1733 |

The thirteen colonies

Americans in the eastern colonies wanted more room, more land, and more opportunities. From the 1600s to the late 1800s pioneers moved steadily westward.

Wagon train on the Oregon Trail

Early pioneers walked or rode on horseback. After trails were blazed, many went by covered wagon. Sometimes many families traveled west together in long lines of wagons known as wagon trains.

Frederic Remington's painting, *The Emigrants*

Whether going to Ohio
in the 1700s or Oregon in
the 1800s, pioneers faced
many hardships. They had
to hunt for food along the
way. When they came to
rivers, they had to find
someone with a raft or

23

build their own. When storms struck, they had to find shelter. One terrible problem was illness. Often there were no doctors for hundreds of miles. Of the more than twenty thousand pioneers buried along the Oregon Trail, most died of disease.

The pioneers who reached their goal had no time to rest. First they had to build houses. In forested regions, they chopped down trees and built log

Sod house, photographed near Coburg, Nebraska in 1887

cabins. But in some places—such as Kansas, Nebraska, and the Dakotas—there were no trees. In such places the pioneers cut the hard ground, called sod, into bricks. They used the bricks to build sod houses.

Pioneers in the town of Purcell, Oklahoma in 1889

In places where many pioneers settled, towns were built. The pioneers named the new towns after friends, relatives, and famous people.

As soon as they could, the pioneers planted crops.

*A Prayer for Rain*
by Arthur Burdett Frost

In Iowa and Illinois they grew corn. Wheat was planted in Kansas and the Dakotas. In the South they grew cotton. By finding out which crops grew best in a place, pioneers made life easier for later settlers.

Photograph (left) and engraving (right) show settlers racing to stake their claim to lands in Oklahoma. These lands had been taken from the original settlers—the Indians.

Oklahoma was one of the last places in the United States settled by pioneers. When the U.S. government opened Oklahoma for settlement in 1889, thousands of pioneers headed there. On one day alone—April 22,

1889—fifty thousand pioneers moved into Oklahoma.

By 1900 people had settled across the United States. The country's pioneer days were over. Americans have not forgotten the pioneers, though. Many families still tell stories about their pioneer ancestors. Many towns honor pioneers by preserving their log cabins and other relics.

# A FEW FAMOUS PIONEERS

Eric the Red and his son Leif Ericsson were two famous pioneers. Both were also explorers.

Eric the Red (about A.D. 950 to about A.D. 1003) was born in Norway. In his youth, Eric went to live in Iceland. After getting into several fights, Eric was thrown out of Iceland for three years.

Eric the Red discovered Greenland.

Eric sailed west and settled on an island. The island was ice covered, but upon returning to Iceland Eric described it as a "green land" because he wanted people to live there with him. About 985

Eric did return to present-day Greenland with some pioneers. They built a colony that lasted for several hundred years.

Leif Ericsson (about A.D. 980 to about A.D. 1025) went even farther west than his father. Around the year 1000 he and a group of pioneers sailed west from Greenland. They landed somewhere in North America—probably in Canada. As far as is

Leif Ericsson was the first European to land in North America.

known, they were the first
Europeans to land on the
mainland of the Americas.

At a place they called
Vinland, Ericsson and his
men built a settlement.
During the 1960s ruins of
an ancient settlement were

found in Newfoundland,
Canada. It may be the one
built by Leif Ericsson and
his fellow pioneers a
thousand years ago.

Another very famous
pioneer, Daniel Boone
(1734-1820), loved hunting
and going to new places.

In 1775 Boone blazed a
trail from Virginia to
central Kentucky. This trail
was called the Wilderness
Road. He built the town
of Boonesborough where

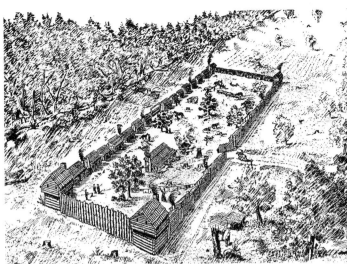

Daniel Boone (left) and
Fort Boonesborough (right)
Boone built this fort at the end
of the Wilderness Road.

the trail ended and brought
his family to live there.

Daniel Boone had many
adventures in Kentucky. He
was captured by Indians
several times. He and his

men had to defend Boonesborough against Indian attack. However, his big gift to the region was the Wilderness Road. Hundreds of thousands of pioneers used it to move west. Daniel Boone later lived in West Virginia and Missouri.

Davy Crockett (1786-1836), born in Tennessee, was a pioneer, hunter, Indian fighter, and lawmaker. He also was

Davy Crockett (left) and
an engraving of a pioneer
homestead on the western frontier
in 1847

living proof that pioneers
were smart people. Many
of his sayings—such as
"Be sure you are right,
then go ahead."—are
repeated to this day. Davy
Crockett was killed at the

Pioneer and
missionary
Marcus Whitman

Alamo while fighting for
the independence of Texas.
Marcus Whitman (1802-
1847) and his wife,
Narcissa Whitman (1808-
1847), were born in
New York State. They were

Whitman's Old Mission House

missionaries—persons who travel to spread religion. In 1836 the Whitmans moved across the country to what is now Washington State. They built a mission near present-day Walla Walla, Washington. There they taught the Indians about farming and the Christian religion. The Whitmans also encouraged more settlers to come to the region.

The Indians grew angry at the white settlers, including the Whitmans. Not only had the settlers taken land, they also had brought diseases that killed many Indians. In 1847, Indians killed Marcus and Narcissa Whitman and twelve others at the mission.

# THE NATIVE PEOPLE

It takes great courage to settle in unknown lands. That is why American pioneers are considered to be heroes. Yet there is a sad part to the story of American pioneers. As they

Breaking land on the Midwest prairie

arrived, the people who
had been in America
first—the Indians—were
pushed off their lands.

Often, the Indians were
cheated out of their lands
by legal papers called
treaties. Indians who fought
for their lands were called
savages and defeated in
wars.

The story of the Indians
is not unusual. Time and

Colored engraving of fur traders on the
Missouri River being attacked by Indians

again, pioneers have
pushed the natives off the
land. People who have
been forced to leave their
homes don't call the
newcomers "pioneers."
They call them "invaders."

# THE FUTURE OF PIONEERING

Future pioneers may go to live on far-off worlds. If the earth gets too crowded, this may be necessary.

Although they will travel farther, space pioneers will do what pioneers have always done. They will pack their belongings, say good-bye to their friends, and leave home. Once on the new worlds they will

Space colony

build homes and find ways to make a living. They will have one big advantage over all past pioneers, though. They'll be able to tell some out-of-this-world pioneering stories to their grandchildren!

# WORDS YOU SHOULD KNOW

**ancestors**(AN • sess • terz) — relatives from the distant past

**coast**(COHST) — the land along a large body of water

**colonize**(KOL • uh • nyze) — to establish a settlement outside a people's home country

**colony**(KOL • uh • nee) — a settlement built by a people outside their home country

**discover**(diss • KUV • er) — to find out about something before anyone else does

**explorers**(x • PLOR • erz) — people who visit and study unknown lands

**history**(HISS • tor • ee) — a record of events

**independence**(in • dih • PEN • denss) — freedom

**invaders**(in • VAID • erz) — unwanted newcomers

**language**(LANG • widj) — the set of words used by a people

**million**(MILL • yun) — a thousand thousand (1,000,000)

**missionaries**(MISH • un • air • eez) — persons who travel in order to spread religion

**natives**(NAY • tivz) — people who have made a particular place their home for a long time

**opportunity**(op • er • TOON • it • ee) — the chance to make things better

**permanent**(PERM • ah • nent) — something that is lasting

**pioneers**(pie • oh • NEERZ) — persons who are among to the first to move into a region

**prehistoric**(pre • hiss • TORE • ick) — belonging to the time before written history

**religion**(re • LIJ • un) — a set of beliefs concerning God

**ruins**(ROO • inz) — the remains of something

**settlement**(SET • il • ment) — a small village or town

**settlers**(SET • lerz) — people who have come to live in an area

**sod**(SAWD) — grass-covered ground

**treaty**(TREET • ee) — an agreement made to promote peace

**wagon train**(WAG • un TRAYN) — a long line of wagons headed in the same direction

# INDEX

## About the Author

*Dennis Fradin attended Northwestern University on a partial creative writing scholarship and graduated in 1967. He has published stories and articles in such places as* Ingenue, The Saturday Evening Post, Scholastic, Chicago, Oui, *and* National Humane Review. *His previous books include the Young People's Stories of Our States series for Childrens Press, and* Bad Luck Tony *for Prentice-Hall. In the True book series Dennis has written about astronomy, farming, comets, archaeology, movies, the space lab, explorers, and pioneers. He is married and the father of three children.*